Tech

Based on

Mari … res

Ginn

Ginn

Ginn is an imprint of Pearson Education Limited, a company
incorporated in England and Wales, having its registered office
at Edinburgh Gate, Harlow, Essex, CM20 2JE.
Registered company number: 872828

Visit www.ginn.co.uk to see a chart showing you all the Pocket Reads programme information you will need.

From the Spinouts project developed by Paul Collins and Meredith Costain.

14
10 9 8 7 6
ISBN 978 0 602242 59 6

Illustrated by Terry Denton and Phil Garner
Cover illustration by Marc McBride
Designed by Carolyn Gibson
Repro by Digital Imaging, Glasgow
Printed and bound in China (GCC/06)

Marianne de Pierres

Marianne de Pierres lives in Australia with her husband, three sons and any passing koalas. She has the best fun writing stories for children, but sometimes she gets very serious and writes novels for adults as well. Visit Marianne's website at www.mariannedepierres.com.

About the story

"My sons get so involved with their computer games I sometimes think they'd like to be inside them. Which would be OK, as long as you were sure you could get out again ..."

Marianne de Pierres

CHAPTER 1

DO NOT USE THIS COMPUTER IF YOUR HANDS ARE STICKY!

Everyone liked Mellor. He was cool, he was clever, and he was good at football.

He also had a fantastic computer. It came from the Wacky Weird Science Company.

Mellor's computer looked like a spaceship, and it had all the best games. One day, he took it to school. He let everyone play on it. Well, everyone except Cheesel Burg.

Cheesel loved to eat crisps and snacks. No one liked him much.

"It's not fair," Cheesel said to Mellor. "I never get to go on your computer."

"That's because your hands are always sticky," said Mellor. He showed Cheesel a notice that came with the computer.

DO NOT USE THIS COMPUTER IF YOUR HANDS ARE STICKY!

(Especially if they have chocolate on them.)

From the Wacky Weird Science Company.

"Huh!" said Cheesel. "Have it your own way, then." But he had an idea.

After school, when Mellor was playing football, Cheesel went back into the classroom. He had a packet of his favourite crisps – the new chocolate-covered ones.

Cheesel saw Mellor's computer on the table. He opened it up and clicked to start the *Demon Wizard* game. Then he waited.

While he waited, Cheesel ate some crisps. The chocolate got all over his hands.

Then the game asked him to type his name. He typed: C H E E S ...

"Oops!" said Cheesel. "Chocolate all over the computer ... Aaaaargh!"

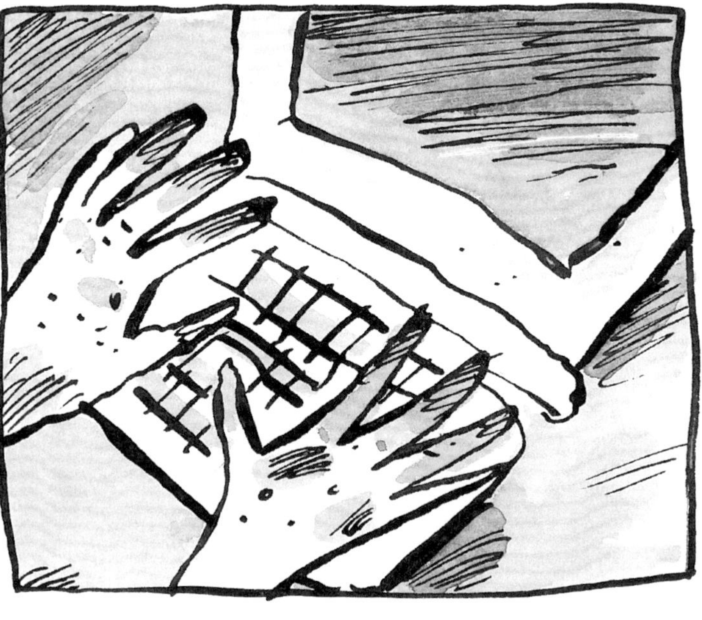

CHAPTER 2

Watch Out – Here Comes Master Bad!

After football, Mellor went to get his computer.

"That's odd," he said to himself. "The computer's on!" On the screen Mellor could see the Demon Wizard's servant, Master Bad.

Master Bad was stuck still. He was about to throw a thunderbolt at …

"Cheesel!" shouted Mellor. In the corner of the screen, a tiny person was jumping about. It was Cheesel!

Then Mellor saw the chocolate all over his computer. "Cheesel!" he shouted again. "Look at the mess you made!"

On the screen, tiny Cheesel sat down and put his head in his hands.

"How did you get in there?" asked Mellor. He wiped the chocolate off the computer. At once, Master Bad started moving. The thunderbolt flew towards Cheesel. Cheesel ran to hide in the forest near the Demon Wizard's castle. Master Bad chased after him, throwing more thunderbolts.

There was only one thing for Mellor to do. He took a crisp from the packet, and rubbed his sticky fingers on the computer. In a flash, the classroom changed to a forest. Mellor was in the computer game!

CHAPTER 3

Thunderbolts and Lightning

Wow!

Mellor could hardly believe it. He was right next to the moat of the Wizard's castle!

There was a flash of lightning, and Master Bad appeared.

Mellor ran to the moat and put his hands in the water. The moat was full of blue energy fish. Mellor got hold of one of the fish and ate it. It wriggled in his throat like a big worm.

Master Bad started to throw thunderbolts, but suddenly Mellor had a shield around him. The thunderbolts bounced back at Master Bad, who disappeared in a ball of smoke.

"He must have gone to Level Two," thought Mellor.

Mellor ran to the forest, where he found Cheesel hiding under a gillberry bush. Cheesel was shaking like a jelly.

"Mellor?" said Cheesel as he crawled out from the bush. "I'm really sorry!"

"Oh well," said Mellor. "We're here now – and it's kind of cool. I suppose we have to beat Master Bad to get out."

"But I'm no good at games!" Cheesel wailed. "I'll get zapped!"

"Hopefully," Mellor agreed.

Cheesel looked as if he was going to cry. Suddenly, Mellor felt sorry for him.

"Here! Eat as many of these as you can." Mellor ate a handful of gillberries, and gave some to Cheesel.

Full of gillberry power, Mellor and Cheesel ran through the forest.

They came to a huge wall with a ladder against it. "We're going up to Level Two!" shouted Mellor. He bounded up the ladder, with Cheesel right behind him.

CHAPTER 4

Moat Mongos

Level Two was harder than Level One. To beat Master Bad, you had to get to the castle by crossing the drawbridge over the moat.

Cheesel and Mellor walked towards the castle.

"Er – what happens now?" asked Cheesel.

"We have to defeat the Moat Mongos," said Mellor.

"M-m-m-moat Mongos? What are they?" asked Cheesel. "They sound s-s-s-scary!"

"They are huge mud monsters with tentacles," said Mellor. "They live in the moat."

"O-oh," said Cheesel quietly.

At last they reached the drawbridge. The moat looked very peaceful.

"Can't we just run over the drawbridge?" asked Cheesel.

Mellor shook his head. "Watch this." He picked up a stone and threw it onto the middle of the drawbridge. Quick as a wink, a tentacle snaked out. It dragged the stone into the water.

"That could be us," said Mellor.

"What are we going to do?" wailed Cheesel.

"We will have to steal Master Bad's sword," said Mellor, bravely. "Or rather – **you** will."

"Me?" squeaked Cheesel.

"I'll distract Master Bad," said Mellor. "You creep up behind him. Grab the sword and stick it in the moat. The power from the sword will zap the Moat Mongos. Then we can cross the drawbridge." And away he ran, after Master Bad.

"Brilliant," said Cheesel, very quietly indeed.

CHAPTER 5

Press Save!

When Master Bad saw Mellor, he started throwing thunderbolts. Mellor was in big trouble. "Hurry up, Cheesel!" he shouted.

Suddenly, Cheesel had an idea. "I could be a hero!" he said to himself. "Then everyone would like me!" He crept up to the drawbridge, behind Master Bad.

Cheesel reached out for Master Bad's sword. Just then, a tentacle shot out towards him.

Cheesel bumped into Master Bad. The sword fell out of Master Bad's hand … and into the water. There was a huge flash of blue light, and the game disappeared.

Cheesel found himself standing back in the classroom. He was dripping with water. Mellor's computer was in front of him.

But where was Mellor?

Cheesel looked at the screen. There was Mellor, jumping about and shouting.

"I'm stuck in *Save Game*," yelled Mellor. "Press Save!"

"Oh," said Cheesel. "Sure."

Then he saw the packet of crisps. There was just one crisp left – an extra chocolatey one. Cheesel picked up the crisp and put it in his mouth. There was chocolate all over his fingers.

He reached out and touched the computer ...

THE END?